THE OLD ONES

A Children's Book About
The Cliff Dwellers

Text and Photographs by:
Brian Freeman & Jodi Freeman

Drawings by:
Terry Flanagan

The authors extend thanks to Linda Martin, Rovilla Ellis, Robert Heyder, Jack Muller, Don Fiero, Dabney Ford, Phill Hecker, Tom Vaughan, Kathy Fiete, David Noble, Peter Pino, and Victor Jackson for their invaluable assistance.

Special thanks to Ruth James for blazing the trail and Terry Flanagan for adding her valuable, artistic touch.

The Old Ones: A Children's Book About the Cliff Dwellers, Third Edition. Text and Photographs by Brian Freeman & Jodi Freeman. Drawings by Terry Flanagan.

Published by: **THE THINK SHOP INC.** & *First Light* PUBLISHING
1813 E. Mulberry Street
Fort Collins, CO 80524
(970)224-1579

Printed in the United States

ISBN 1-889459-06-2

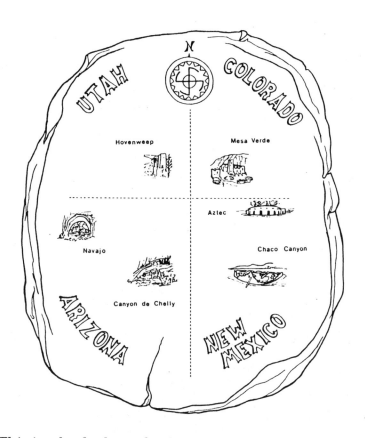

This is a book about the Anasazi Indians. Anasazi is a Navajo Indian word that means Old Ones. People today are still learning more about the Anasazi's lives. The Anasazi did not leave any written information. People study things the Old Ones left behind. They also learn about them from the Hopi and Pueblo Indians today. It is a lot like doing a puzzle without knowing what the picture is. When you read this book, remember one thing . . . it's hard to know anything for sure. No one was there a thousand years ago. This book will tell you what many people think is true. But the experts disagree about many things.

Canyon de Chelley National Monument, Arizona

The Old Ones lived in different places in the Southwest. Some lived on the mesas. Some lived in canyons. Others lived in the desert.

Mesa Verde National Park, Colorado

Chaco Culture National Historical Park,
New Mexico

This is what the Anasazi children saw when they looked out this door. From other doors, they might have seen people working. What do you see when you look out your door?

The Anasazi children did not have the kind of toys
you have. They probably climbed trees, sang songs,
played games, and listened to stories. Do you like to do
these things?

There was a lot of work to do. When the children
weren't playing, they probably helped with the work.

When you need something, you go to the store. The Old Ones didn't have any stores. They had to make everything they needed. They used plants and animal skins to make their clothes.

In the summer, they might have worn aprons and sandals. They made these from the strings of yucca plants.

In the winter, they made robes and blankets from yucca strings. They wove in turkey feathers or rabbit fur to make the clothes warm. They also used animal skins to make winter clothes.

Would you like to make all of your clothes? Many people enjoy making their clothes.

The yucca plant was used for many other things. The fruit from the yucca was eaten for food. They may have used the roots to make shampoo, like the later Indians did.

Piñon tree

Piñon trees were very important. They burned the wood to keep warm. The piñon nuts were good to eat. The sap was used for glue. They also put sap on their baskets so they could carry water in them. The wood was sometimes used to make the roofs of the Indians' houses.

Yucca fruit

The Anasazi lived 1000 years before there were gro-
cery stores. They *never* had hamburgers, pizza, cake,
candy, ice cream, or pop! They spent most of their time
hunting for food. They ate fruit from plants like the
yucca and the prickly pear cactus. They also found
seeds, berries, and nuts to eat.

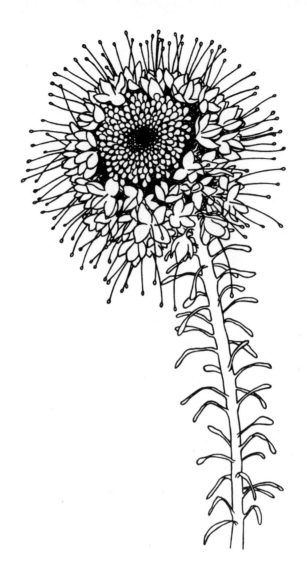

Bee Flowers

There were a lot of pretty flowers. Some were very useful. The Old Ones ate bee flowers. They cooked the flower and the leaves. They ate seeds from sunflowers.

Sunflowers

Poison Ivy and Cactus

Not everything about the plants was useful. Do you suppose the Anasazi children ever fell on any cactus? Do you think they got poison ivy like children do today?

We get most of our meat from cows, pigs and chickens. The Anasazi did not have these animals. They ate mice, squirrels, gophers, rabbits, mountain sheep, and deer. Some people think they ate turkeys, but no one knows for sure. They used a spear to hunt the big animals. They caught the little animals with a net.

Deer

The Anasazi saw a lot of wild animals every day. They saw bugs, toads, lizards, snakes, deer, and many others. What kind of animals do you see every day?

Horned Toad

Collared Lizard

The first Anasazi spent a lot of time traveling to look for food. They did not stay long in the same place. They did not have time to build houses. They spent the nights in small caves or under cliffs.

These people are called Basket Makers. Why do you think people call them that? The women were very good at making baskets. Sometimes they cut their hair and used it in the baskets they made! Would you do that? I bet your family wouldn't like it if you did.

They used baskets to cook their food. They could not cook over a fire with a straw basket. The women were smart. They took hot stones from the fire. Then they put the stones in the basket. The hot stones cooked their food! Would you like to cook that way, or would you rather eat your food raw?

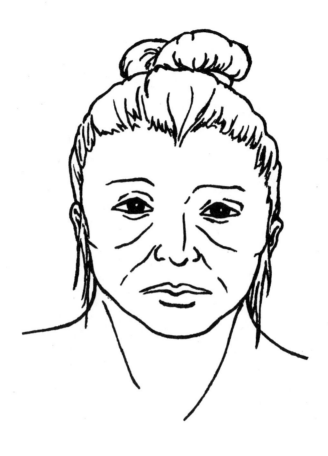

The men probably didn't cut their hair to weave into baskets. They may have had long, fancy hair styles. The Old Ones made combs with bones and feathers. They wore combs in their hair. Sometimes they wore their hair in buns.

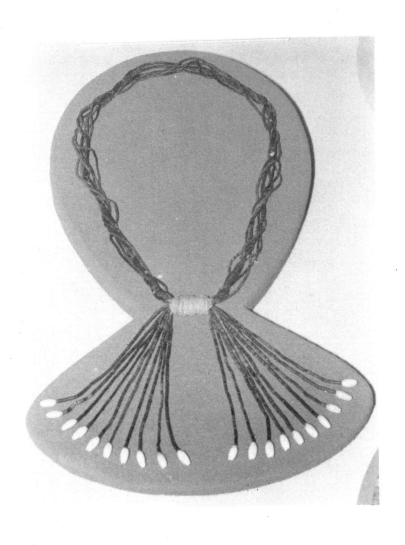

The Old Ones liked jewelry. They made necklaces, earrings, and hair combs. They made their jewelry with bones, stones, shells, and feathers. One necklace had 2500 beads. How many beads would you string to make your necklace?

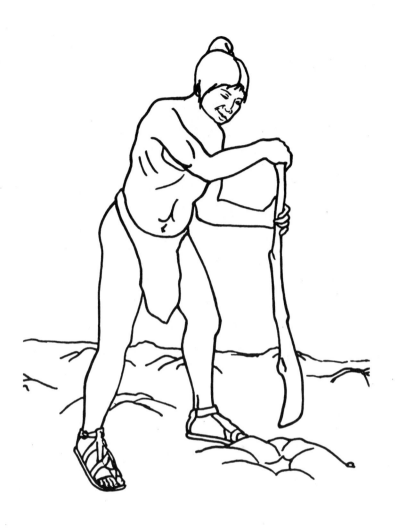

After a while, the Anasazi learned to raise corn, beans, and squash. They used a digging stick to plant the seeds.

The women made corn meal by grinding the corn between two stones. These stones are called a mano and metate. The rubbing of the stones also made sand. Would you like sand in your food? The sand wore out the Indians' teeth.

The Anasazi did not have all the kinds of food they needed. About all they had to eat was meat, corn, beans, squash, nuts, berries, and greens. And there were no doctors to help sick people. Most of them only lived to be about 34 years old!

The Basket Makers hunted with spears for about 500 years. Then they learned to make bows and arrows. Would you rather hunt with a spear or a bow and arrow? A bow and arrow is easier to aim and it is more powerful. This helped them to be better hunters. Now the Basket Makers did not have to spend so much time looking for food.

The Basket Maker women learned to make simple pottery. The pottery made it easier to cook food. They did not have to put hot stones in the pots. Now they could cook dinner over a fire. The food cooked faster and tasted better.

The later Basket Makers did not travel as much as the first Basket Makers. They had to stay home and take care of the corn, beans, and squash.

They began to build very simple houses. They dug round holes in the ground. They didn't have shovels. How would you dig a hole without a shovel?

The Old Ones used logs and sticks to make walls and a roof. They had to work hard to cut logs with a stone ax. They covered the walls and sticks with mud.

Some houses had a door in the side. Others had a hole in the roof for the door. They used a ladder to go in and out. How do you think they kept rain and snow from coming in the door? Would you like a door in the roof of your house?

The Basket Makers' houses were called pit houses. They were cool in the summer. In the winter, the Old Ones built fires to keep warm. What problems do you think they had with a campfire in their house? Some pithouses caught fire, and there were no firemen to call!

The Indian women had a lot of work to do. They didn't have day care or babysitters, so they put their babies on cradleboards. Then the babies could go everywhere with their mothers. What do you think of this idea?

They didn't have diapers like ours. The mothers may have crushed soft bark from Juniper trees to use for a diapers. This is what the later Indians did.

The Hopi Indians are the great grandchildren of the
Anasazi. Their stories say that the Anasazi women
owned the houses that the men built. Sometimes, a
woman got mad at her husband and wanted a divorce.
She set his things outside the door. Then he had to
leave. Some people don't think this is true. We don't
know for sure. There are no Anasazi left to tell us!

After 200 years, the Old Ones changed their pit-houses. They started building square houses on top of the ground. They would build them all in a row like some apartment buildings today. These houses were called pueblos. Now the Old Ones are called Pueblo People.

The Old Ones still made rooms in the ground. These rooms were almost like pithouses, but they are called kivas.

The first kivas were small and simple. Later, they built kivas like the ones in the pictures. Most kivas were round, but a few were square. Some were big, but most were small. Each kiva had a firepit to keep them warm. Some kivas had a sipapu hole. The Old Ones believed that man first came to earth through a sipapu hole.

People think kivas were like a church and like a club house. Kivas were probably for men. The women may have come in at special times.

A big kiva - Chaco Canyon

A small kiva - Mesa Verde

Anasazi women got very good at making pots. They made bowls, cups, ladles, and lots of other things. They did not make as many baskets now. Why do you think they liked pots better than baskets? The Anasazi made paint so they could put lines and pictures on their pots. Do you think they did a good job?

DOUBLE MUG

DONOR MR. W. D. EWING, DURANGO, COLO.

35

The women didn't need to use their hair to make pottery, like they did when they made baskets. They let their hair grow long.

Water is very important. Why did the Anasazi need water? They needed it to drink. Sometimes, they only had a little tiny bit of water from springs like the one above. Then they barely had enough water to drink. They could not waste water. They may not have been able to take a bath very often. Would you like that?

Some rocks held large puddles after a rain. This helped the Old Ones save water for the dry times. Would you like to drink water from a puddle? What if it was the only water you could get?

The Old Ones grew most of their food on top of the mesas. But some years it didn't rain very much.

When it didn't rain much, the Anasazi had ways to catch the rain. They built little terraces in ditches. The terraces looked like big steps going down the hill. They had some plants growing on each step. When it rained, the water ran into the ditch. This is how they watered their plants during the dry years. They also grew plants that didn't need much water.

Mummy Lake, Mesa Verde National Park

The Anasazi at Mesa Verde tried to build a man-made lake. They wanted to have enough water for everyone. They built a round stone wall. They built ditches to bring in the water. People make lakes today by building dams that block rivers.

Cliff Palace, Mesa Verde National Park

About 800 years ago, some of the Anasazi decided to live in cliffs. Others decided to build big "apartment" houses at the bottom of the cliffs. Many houses were small. 1000 people may have lived in the biggest houses. Some cities may have had 6000 people. But no one knows for sure.

Pueblo Bonito, Chaco Culture National
Historical Park, New Mexico

A small dwelling, Mesa Verde National Park

White House Ruin,
Canyon de Chelley National Monument

Long House Ruin, Mesa Verde National Park

Holly Ruin

Hovenweep National Monument

Keet Seel, Navajo National Monument

Kin Kletso, Chaco Culture National
Historical Park, New Mexico

The people built walls in many different ways. Most of the walls were made with stone. Others were made with sticks and mud. You can still see the fingerprints of the Old Ones in the mud walls of some buildings.

These houses looked more like apartments you see today. But they were very different. They had no TV's. They had no lights. They had no stereos. There was no refrigerator. They did not have furniture or a bathroom like ours. Would you like to live that way? The Old Ones lived a long time ago, but there are places in the world where people still live that way today. Some people like to live that way.

The Anasazi's doors were very small. The people were not that little. They were only a few inches shorter than people are today. Their doors were small to keep the warm air in the house. Some of the doors were shaped like our doors and some were shaped like keyholes.

The Anasazi liked to line up their doors and windows all in a row. Sometimes they had to walk through other rooms to get to their room. Would you like your family walking through your room?

Sometimes they closed a door or window with rocks.
Why do you think they did that?

The apartment and cliff houses were crowded. Sometimes there was only three or four rooms for a family. A big family sometimes included the grandparents, parents, children, aunts, uncles, and cousins! Would you like to have a big family living with you?

There were no shelves or cupboards. The Anasazi built small storage rooms to keep food in.

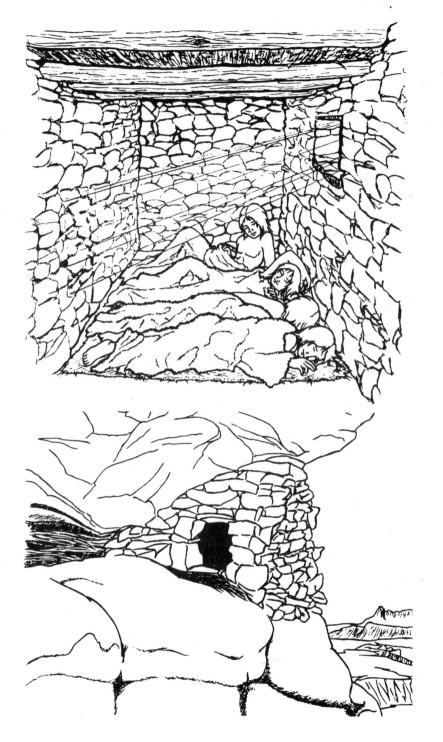

Petroglyph

The Anasazi liked to draw pictures. They did not have any paper, so they made pictures on rock walls! Some pictures were painted on the walls. Others were cut in with stones. This was ok then, but would your family like it if you made pictures on the wall?

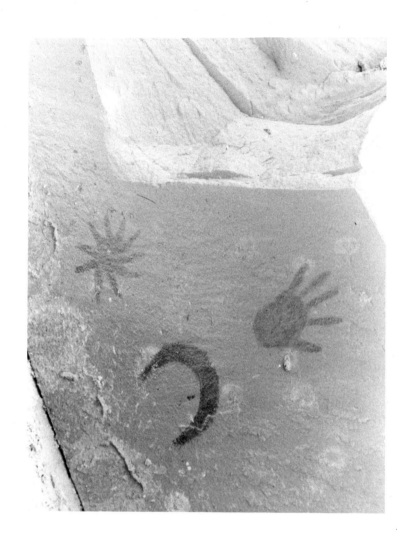

Pictograph

Some of the Anasazi grew food on top of the mesas. Their houses were in the cliffs or on the ground below. How do you think they got up and down the cliff walls? Sometimes they used ladders and tunnels.

In some places, they carved stairs in the rock.

Sometimes they could not build stairs or use ladders. They put little holes and steps in the cliffs. They were just big enough for toes and fingers to hang on. The Old Ones were very good climbers.

Would you like to climb a cliff that way? The Anasazi could carry heavy loads on their backs while they climbed big cliffs!

The Old Ones did not have any horses. They had to walk or run everywhere. They walked some trail so many times that they made deep paths, like the one in the picture.

How far would you go if you had to walk? The Indians did not stay home all the time. Some walked 100 miles to get many different things they wanted. They traded for cotton to make clothes and blankets, or shells for jewelry. Then they carried it 100 miles to get home again. There was no post office to mail anything. What would you walk 200 miles to get?

Some of the Anasazi threw their trash over the cliff. Others used an empty room in the house for a giant trash can.

People learn about the Anasazi by studying their trash. It has things they used and threw away. It tells us about their food, clothes and tools. What would people learn about you if they studied your trash?

The Old Ones lived in their cliff houses less than 100 years. Why do you think they moved again? No one knows for sure. Some people think it was because it didn't rain for 12 or 13 years. It's hard to raise food without rain. Maybe other people came to steal their food. What would you do if someone was stealing your food?

Maybe the Anasazi had worn out the soil and used up the trees. Maybe there were too many people and not enough food. Maybe people got sick and died. No one knows for sure.

We have these same problems today. Some parts of the world have too many people and not enough food. People are using up trees, minerals, and energy.

When the Anasazi used up their resources, they moved to a new place. What will people do today after they use up all the resources? What do you think people should do to solve this problem?

Taos Pueblo, New Mexico

Where did the Old Ones go? They moved to other places in Arizona and New Mexico, where other Indians lived. They built more pueblos. People believe the Hopi and Pueblo Indians of today are the great, grandchildren of the Old Ones. They still build pueblos and apartment houses. Many still have kivas. They have taught us a lot about the Anasazi.